How to Write When Everything Goes Wrong

A Practical Guide to Writing Through Tough Times

by

Allie Pleiter

Other books for writers by Allie Pleiter:

The Chunky Method Handbook:
Your Step-by-Step Plan to WRITE THAT BOOK Even
When Life Gets in the Way

Print ISBN-10: 0-9972982-6-X
Print ISBN-13: 978-0-9972982-6-0

Contents

Introduction

Life, as they say, is what happens while you are making other plans.

Adversity has a way of poking its nasty head into the best of our plans, throwing up obstacles with no regard to our deadlines, desires, or composure. It's never a matter of *if* life is going to mess with your goals; it's only a matter of *when*.

My dearest hope is that you've picked up this book while your life is calm, wisely opting to shore up your creativity vessel for the time when the world "gifts" you with a storm. It's no accident that each chapter has a maritime theme, and that a life ring graces the cover of this book. Indeed, you need to learn how to stay afloat, how to row for shore, how to raise flags to communicate, how to light guiding beacons, etc. But the most essential truth of the maritime metaphor is this: The life ring works best if you remember to keep it on board and on hand *before* your boat leaves the dock.

It is more likely, however, that you've picked up this book because you've already encountered adversity. Worse yet, the storm has just hit, and your boat is rocking...or maybe even sinking. You need those oars and flags and beacons and survival skills *right now*. Somehow you must figure out how to keep your writing going amid all this muse-squashing chaos.

Either way, take heart. Help is on the way in these pages.

Writing Is a Unique Kind of Work

...creative work—the kind of writing that is different from journaling or other therapeutic output—often feels impossible when you are in the midst of disaster.

Real help is necessary because writing isn't like other kinds of productivity. I believe writing takes the same kind of energy required to solve problems or cope with sadness or keep our heads above water through an emotional flood. Physical work, or even tedious work, can sometimes be a balm in times of crisis; but creative work—the kind of writing that is different from journaling or other therapeutic output—often feels impossible when you are in the midst of disaster. I know because I have been there. Here's what you'll learn from this book:

- Practical tips for getting through the thick of your crisis
- Advice from authors who have met their deadlines in the face of monumental challenges (myself included)
- Strategies for communicating with those around you to access help, advice, support, and encouragement
- Counsel from writers who learned when

and how to throw up a white flag (myself included again)

- Tips on when and how to write about the crisis you are going through—because, as they say, "It's all material"
- Insights into how your natural storytelling ability both helps and hinders your recovery
- Methods for looking at your experiences and mining them for the treasures they can bring to your writing
- Guidance on speaking publicly about your challenges, especially regarding how to separate the useful parts of your trauma from the ones best kept private

Most of all, I hope this book helps you find a strengthened confidence in your own abilities—waterlogged as they may feel at the moment—and encouragement to gather the help you need. No matter what challenge you may be facing, I firmly believe it can lead to a deeper, stronger writing career. You just need your writing vessel to survive the voyage from here to there, and this book is designed to provide the tools.

Ready or not (and believe me, I've spent *lots* of time in the "not" camp), let's launch this voyage.

Chapter 1

Stay Afloat: Survival Tactics

> If you can take steps to
> control and contain your
> crisis, everything else—
> including finding the energy
> to create—gets easier.

We are writers. That creates its own challenges on a good day, much less when life goes awry. So here's the brutal but essential truth: *If you want to write when everything goes wrong, you have to tend to what's wrong in order to write.* In terms of our maritime metaphors, you have to turn your bow into the waves so they stop rocking your boat. If you can take steps to control and contain your crisis, everything else—including finding the energy to create—gets easier.

Writing amid a crisis doesn't just feel nearly impossible. It *is* nearly impossible. So let us first lay out some basic crisis survival skills for the creative person. Don't worry—I promise we will focus on the writing in the next chapter, but first we have to get our heads above water and stay afloat. Here's how.

Tactic 1: Ask Yourself the Powerful Questions

The primary goal in any crisis is to make it out intact: To survive, even if it means nursing new wounds in the process. To keep our sense of hope afloat, even if it exhausts us. To view the light at the end of the tunnel with optimism, even if confidence feels out of reach. We want to keep whatever we are facing from completely derailing us, either in terms of our lives or our creativity.

In a September 2012 blog post, brilliant leadership guru Michael Hyatt suggested facing adversity with the following question: "What does this experience make possible?" I believe Michael's question launches a perspective shift that's crucial to handling a challenge. Taking it a step further, I suggest you ask yourself these four questions when a crisis or setback hits:

A. What's possible now?

When crisis hits, our brains can kick into what's known as totalitarian thinking: Everything's awful, my plans are shot, my life's a mess, etc. It's a perfectly human reaction for the first twenty-four hours after calamity hits—and even longer for devastating events, such as the sudden loss of a family member or spouse. If you can shift your thinking even the smallest bit toward what is still intact, however, you have found your first foothold of survival.

Here's a minor example: A delayed flight forces you to miss a crucial connection, and you will arrive in Phoenix too late to attend a friend's wedding. Ouch. After allowing yourself a few minutes to react—shock, anger, annoyance, frustration—you play a game with yourself: What *is* possible now? Being stuck in an airport can lead to hours of useful work time for the flexible, opportunistic writer. A quiet corner with your laptop or notebook can become a place to draft, outline, plot, research, or edit.

> ## You need to force a shift of thinking to unearth "what's possible now?"

If you find yourself still too steamed to create, do you have time to find a decent meal? Could the airport bookshop have that book you've put off reading? Are there podcasts stored up on your computer or smartphone than can turn those extra hours into educational sessions? Perhaps you could simply discover new friends as you and your fellow stranded passengers bond over scuttled plans.

None of these possibilities will occur to you if you stew in your justified annoyance. You need to force a shift of thinking to unearth "what's possible now?" It is genuinely hard to drag your brain off the negative, but the more you practice this shift, the easier it becomes. In particular, I have found positivity to be contagious in group settings. Think about all those videos that pop up on YouTube about choirs breaking into spontaneous concerts on grounded aircraft. Don't they always make you smile? That's the power of "what's possible now?"

B. What's *not* possible now?

Many of us get into deeper trouble precisely because we refuse to recognize the limitations we face amid a crisis. To go back to our missed flight illustration, what's *not* possible now is attending the Phoenix wedding. That fact needs to be faced, and the sooner the better.

You likely have your own examples of scuttled plans, but here was one of my biggest: Years ago I was a recently graduated theater major bent on a performance career, but I was also suffering regularly from debilitating migraines. My doctor looked me straight in the eye and said, "You may never be able to guarantee your ability to perform as scheduled. That's going to be a problem for what you want to do, and you need to face up to it." Back then we didn't have the great medicines we have now, and those were harsh words. They hurt to hear, but it did help me take a realistic view of which possibilities were open to me and which were not. I would never have become a writer if I'd stubbornly stuck to a career my body wasn't able to embrace. If you've broken your wrist, you likely can't type. If your writing income has dropped to the point where you need to take a temporary job, your writing time may need to take a backseat for a while. Face up to the situation rather than continue in denial. Pretending the situation is better than it is won't do you any favors.

C. What do I *need right now*?

"Right now" is crucial. The first step in any given crisis—once safety concerns have been met, of course—is to get calm. Or at least calm-*er*. You may need to talk to someone who understands the process ahead of you better than you do at the moment. (This is especially true in medical crises.) If you just lost your job, you may need to assess your financial status and determine how long you can hold out without a paycheck. This is a place where being a writer is a liability: our writer brains gallop off into a dozen long-term scenarios, churning today's problems into tomorrow's catastrophes. That's not helpful, because your best hope for results and accommodations often lies in identifying immediate needs. You need to quickly turn your bow into the waves to stop the rocking.

> ...being a writer is a liability: our writer brains gallop off into a dozen long-term scenarios, churning today's problems into tomorrow's catastrophes.

Here's another example: My mother died suddenly in 2000. She was my last surviving parent, so her death brought a host of estate, financial, and logistical issues. The day before her wake, I called a friend who had lost her own mom, desperately wanting to talk to someone who had experienced what I was feeling. She wisely asked me, "What do you need right now?"

What I needed was an attorney, and some financial and real estate advice. I needed a month or more to clear out her house for sale. I needed to worry about my own health, considering I'd lost yet another parent to heart disease. All were valid long-term concerns, but none could be solved immediately as I sat alone in my mother's house that afternoon. I needed *some* solutions if I couldn't get *all* the solutions.

As it turns out, other needs were more pressing. I needed to know my brother's support and companionship were on the way. I needed coffee to stay awake (after a long, sleepless night and a difficult plane ride), and I needed to eat a decent meal. These were all things I could do something about *now*! Meeting those three immediate needs—calling my brother, heading to the coffee shop, swinging by the grocery store—turned my bow into the waves. It grounded me enough to begin finding solutions to the larger issues. It helped me shut down my "what if?" continually plotting writer brain and think in immediate, concrete steps.

> Successful coping comes with tamping down our drastic artist natures (a generalization, yes, but you know how we writers get) and focusing on the next solvable step.

Steer clear of what one writer friend calls "martyr mode"—not eating, hydrating, or sleeping—and address your short-term needs. Most crises must be solved one day at a time, one step at a time, often with the help of others. Successful coping comes with tamping down our drastic artist natures (a generalization, yes, but you know how we writers get) and focusing on the next solvable step.

D. What do I *want* right now?

Resist the urge to think of crisis as a survival state where only needs apply and wants must wait until later. You may *need* to eat, but you may also *want* a friend to help you talk through your situation. You may be stuck in a hospital room with an ill loved one, but you may want a book or magazine (or in my case, a knitting project) to occupy your mind so it doesn't go whizzing off in a dozen disastrous directions. You may want a few moments of peace and quiet to gather your thoughts. You may want a laptop or notebook nearby to write about everything you are feeling. These are not "luxuries" to be cast aside until life calms down. Think about nonessentials that might make you calmer, more comfortable, more in control, or a bit more cheerful. This is *not* selfish. On the contrary, it is a form of self-care that will bolster your endurance or clarity at a time when you need it most.

> Think about nonessentials that might make you calmer, more comfortable, more in control, or a bit more cheerful.

Much of this book was borne from the time my son faced multiple health issues in his early teens. He is a healthy, thriving college student as of this printing, but those half-dozen years of on-and-off medical crises taught me a lot about myself and my ability to cope both as a mother and a writer. Our first and longest hospital stay followed a shocking cancer diagnosis. I quickly realized that the extrovert in me was getting *very* lonely *very* fast. I *needed* to be with my son (and my husband needed to be at work), but the specter of cancer loomed large and dark, bearing loads of information and emotions to process. I craved a friendly face and conversation, so I asked a friend to arrange a daily visitor for me. Not tons of time—just an hour or so—to connect with a human being who wasn't either my son or a medical professional. (I was connecting with both of those on a near-constant basis!) Were those friendly visits a medical necessity? Not really. Useful, uplifting, and supportive? Absolutely. The visits enabled me to find just enough emotional fortitude to do a small amount of writing each day. (More on that later—I promise.)

Your answers to these four questions can provide a needed foothold to get through the first hours or days of any crisis. Though I gave you some pretty drastic examples, I find these questions work for any size dilemma—from a flat tire to a fiscal meltdown. If you can shift your thinking from the knee jerk of *Emergency! Panic!* to identifying what's possible now and what's *not* possible now, then you can act on what you need and want amid the stress of the moment. With these four answers, you have the first steps forward.

Tactic 2: Change What You Can

Human nature wants to transform the bad stuff to good—to remove the discomfort and anxiety and make it "all better." The problem with most crises is that the ones that really knock us off our feet don't have a ready-made "good as new."

> ...every step you take toward improvement gets you closer to the emotional stability that lets you write.

Yes, big problems require complex solutions; but according to wellness expert Dr. John J. Pelizza, in almost every situation—even ones as desperate as terminal illness or war or disability—*something* can often be done to achieve "better." Not "all better," mind you, but some form of incremental improvement. Pain may not be removable, but it can be reduced. An elderly parent may not have hopes of recovering, but they can be made more comfortable. Your house may have been devastated by a flood, but you can find clean clothes to wear. (The ingenious Tide Loads of Hope mobile laundry program was built on this concept.) You may have to look hard, get creative, and ask for help, but there is *almost always* something within your control to improve your situation or environment. And that's crucial, because every step you take toward improvement gets you closer to the emotional stability that lets you write.

For me, the most powerful example came in the form of pajamas. Any person who has spent even four hours in a hospital bed knows the soul-sucking nature of hospital gowns. They are institutional. No one looks comfortable in them. No one feels calm or at home in them. The infamous gap in the back may help a nurse examine you, but it can drive you to distraction. During my son's hospital stay, we were encouraged to bring our own pajamas—both of us. It sounds like a small detail, but I was astounded by the power of having my own PJs. Face it—nothing feels more like a crisis than sleeping in your clothes while your son lies nearby in some icky cotton kimono. Pajamas from home were personal and comfortable. They looked, felt, and even smelled like home. Wearing them gave us an easy-to-implement, tiny slice of power to change our difficult surroundings. And yes, that small burst of strength enabled me to find thirty minutes every day to write two or three pages.

Once you've asked and answered the four questions from the previous section, go change what you can. Are you stranded in an airport? Go find the comfiest chairs or research the cost of a one-day admission to the VIP lounge where you might get some writing done. Have you broken your leg? Find pants that can accommodate your cast and a good laptop desk to turn your chair into an office. Seek out some cheery socks that cover your chilly, bruised toes in style. You may be tempted to say, "That won't solve the problem!"—which is true. It won't solve the problem. But small comforts may make the current situation just a bit more tolerable, and that goes a long way toward getting your creative self into gear.

> The sum total of many small improvements can restore your creative spirit and encourage your ability to write.

Now, I'm no Pollyanna. I understand that you may find yourself in the midst of a situation that will *never* go away. Some losses are permanent; some situations forever change the course of your life. Even so, I believe the above concepts apply. Resisting the temptation to throw your hands up in despair is a worthwhile effort because "better" is still possible. The long-term nature of the challenge makes incremental improvements all the more powerful and necessary.

No matter what your situation, try these principles. Embrace the belief that while "all good" often eludes us, "a little bit better" is possible. The sum total of many small improvements can restore your creative spirit and encourage your ability to write.

Tactic 3: Classify Your Crisis

Writers under fire can sort most crises into one of two categories: *short-term intense* and *long-term epic*. Some problems thrust themselves into our lives and wreak havoc for a day or a week, while others shift our lives for months, years, or forever. Crises make different demands of us and our creativity, and different circumstances require different coping strategies.

A. The short-term intense crisis.

You broke your leg in four places. A tree crashed through your living room. A member of your family is having emergency surgery or has become critically ill. You or your spouse has just been laid off. Such crises attack with little warning, but they have—hopefully—a foreseeable end. It's hard to stay calm and keep the creativity flowing in the midst of a short-term intense crisis because everything is coming at you at once. Here are a few coping strategies.

i. Clear the decks. Get rid of all nonessential commitments *immediately*. Excuse yourself from volunteer committees, critique groups, adjunct projects, and any events that offer more stress than joy. Someone else can run the class holiday party or post this week's blog installment. You only have so much energy and focus. The combination of this new crisis and any writing will take most—if not all—of the energy you've got, leaving no room for extra commitments. If you have trouble saying no to people, enlist the help of a friend or spouse to make those phone calls. Have you scheduled any engagements with people who love you and can offer you encouragement and support? By all means, keep those on your calendar.

ii. Say YES. People will offer to help. Take them up on

it! All of them! When someone offers to pick up your son from school, giving you twenty extra minutes to write (or maybe to just catch your breath), say yes. Accept any and all offers of food, even if it means stocking your fridge with endless macaroni casseroles. The only thing worse than a crisis is a crisis with an empty fridge, and the twenty fewer minutes it takes to heat up a premade casserole rather than cook it could mean a page gets written. Take a half hour and make a list of thirty—yes, thirty—things you need done so you stand a chance of carving out time to write. Be selfish and wimpy. People genuinely want to help, and now is no time to be all strong and independent. Tamp down your inner control freak and let someone else do things for you, even if they do them imperfectly. When you give friends and associates specific, helpful things they can do, you give yourself the gift of watching how much you mean to the people around you. Nothing could be more valuable at a time of crisis than that sense of community support.

> ...make a list of thirty—yes,
> thirty—things you need done
> so you stand a chance of
> carving out time to write.

---

iii. Find a survivor. Locate a writer who has successfully come out the other side of your crisis and make contact with them. Our psyches need hard evidence to counteract all the bad what-ifs our imaginations can dream up. Find a writer whose layoff led to an even better job or gave them time to finally finish that book. Find someone who has recovered from whatever injury or illness you are facing. Some medicines, for example, can mess with a writer's much-needed creativity—but another survivor may recognize symptoms and have solutions to help you on your journey. Give yourself solid reasons to know this won't last forever.

When my son was sick, I was desperate to talk to parents whose children had recovered from each of the four illnesses he faced. Now that he's healthy, I often serve as the "survivor resource" to others. For me personally, it was also important to talk to parents who did not get a happy ending. I needed to meet writers who found a way to write again after the devastating loss of burying a child.

> Facts are useful, but having a name and a story to back up those facts gives them true power for us storytellers.

Ask on social media, check with your doctor or a local support group, utilize outplacement firms, ask friends, or find an online forum; connections are more available now than ever before. Facts are useful, but having a name *and a story* to back up those facts gives them true power for us storytellers. It helps us believe that good outcomes—or even just plain old survival—are possible endings for our story as well.

iv. Assign a manager. Your energies are swallowed up in dealing with whatever crisis you are facing. Especially if you are the patient, coping may take every brain cell you've got, along with all the courage you can muster. You can't afford to divert precious spiritual, emotional, and physical resources to gathering help. That's why you need someone plugging your friends, family, and community into roles of assistance. If administration and organization aren't your gifts (or even if they are), you need a friend who's a master of mustering the troops. Most of us have a friend like this— the one who's always organizing outings, the room mom, the scoutmaster, the volunteer committee chair. Get him or her on board. Give her the task of freeing you up for thirty minutes or an hour to write however many times a week you feel you need it. Take the list you created and send all "How can I help?" inquiries her way. There are even websites like Lotsa Helping Hands set up to digitize assistance, so that even an out-of-town aunt can serve in this role. You'll end up with a team ready to help you find the time to reconnect with your creativity.

These four tactics will take care of basic needs while you deal with whatever catastrophe has befallen you. By enlisting these supports, you'll be able to channel all your time, energy, and focus toward where they need to go: coping. It's okay to be "greedy" for help. Right now, you need it. After all, drastic times call for drastic measures to keep a writer from derailing.

It's okay to be "greedy" for help. Right now, you need it.

23

B. The long-term epic crisis.

Some challenges aren't so drastic in nature, but they are just as daunting. A long-term or chronic illness in you or a close family member changes your life for months, years, or forever. The loss of a loved one is a multiyear journey of grief and adjustment. Your job may be demanding a cross-country move you don't welcome. A beloved pet passes away, or your children go off to college, leaving your house feeling too quiet and too empty to write anything. You may have just discovered you are now the parent of a special needs child. Life can invent a million ways to tilt your world in large-scale and long-suffering ways. We need to be just as inventive and persistent in how we cope and defend our creativity. Here are some important things to remember.

i. Set your pace for distance running. "Don't sprint in a marathon" was the advice our nurse gave to us at the beginning of our son's chemotherapy. We were facing five months of near-daily hospital visits and other exhausting events, and we were tempted to throw up our hands and declare a catastrophe. In many ways, it was—but we were better served by learning survival skills. Getting sleep, eating something other than hospital vending machine food, tending to our daughter's needs as "the one who wasn't sick," and other tasks needed to be done; tending to them kept us afloat and reminded us we were going to be in crisis mode for a very long time. I could no more stop writing on contracted deadlines than my husband could stop going to work at his engineering firm. So we strove for slow and steady pacing, setting reasonable goals that included self-care. To ignore smart pacing would ensure never making it to the finish line.

ii. Look for places to create normalcy. Despite how you may feel at the moment—and how others looking in may view your situation—not every part of your life is blown to bits in a long-term crisis. At first I could not believe what one of our intensive care unit nurses said to us: "You'll be amazed by what you will come to see as a reasonable day." Too often in a long-term crisis we waste energy striving for our old version of normal. We'll find the even keel we need for writing much more easily if we seek ways to create a "new normal"—one adapted to our new circumstances. So ditch the crisis default of sweats, T-shirts, no makeup, and no shower. Instead, take the time to dress normally, keep whatever hours you are used to, watch your favorite shows, have lunch with friends—whatever feels like normal despite your present crazy circumstances.

> We'll find the even keel we need for writing much more easily if we seek ways to create a "new normal"— one adapted to our new circumstances.

I began keeping a half-packed suitcase open and ready during my son's chemotherapy. To see it out in my bedroom became "normal," and it meant my son and I could—and did—calmly pack for a surprise three-day hospital stay in a matter of minutes. We used it dozens of times. And my laptop went in that suitcase every time because writing is part of my normal day. The "sameness" gave us just enough of an edge to keep our sanity amid an insane situation. It became a joke of sorts that the nurses knew to wheel in an extra table so I had a place to write—a near-normal day in a place nowhere near normal.

iii. Take some emotional vitamins. During the marathon of a long-term crisis, a writer needs milestones to break up the seemingly endless stream of cope and compromise and make room for creativity. Don't be afraid to ask friends and family to be generous and frequent with their encouragement. Yes, this may be hard for those of you who hate asking for help. Depression or other circumstances may make reaching out especially difficult, but you need the fuels of praise and support right now. If you embrace the concept of emotional vitamins—daily doses of encouragement to bolster your psychological immune system—you'll be more likely to believe your creativity hasn't left the building for good. Celebration of your first fifteen-minute writing stretch makes it easier to reach for the next one. Find benchmarks—or make them up if you have to—and celebrate them to battle the overwhelm that can be a writer's worst enemy.

> Don't be afraid to ask friends and family to be generous and frequent with their encouragement.

Our most effective "vitamin" came in the form of chocolate cake. A friend who loved to bake made my son a cake and happened to deliver it at the end of his first round of chemo. Because we had cake in the house, we celebrated. The impromptu party gave us all a tremendous boost. Delighted, the dear friend offered to bake another cake at the end of the next round. I cannot overstate the emotional impact of those five cakes, and how they kept me going enough to write. Celebrating even the smallest of victories isn't silly; it's piling up all the positive you can to battle the mounds of negative around you.

Tactic 4: Get Deliberate About Gaining Calm

Calm. It's the thing you desperately need that you can't seem to find in the midst of a crisis. In order to stay creative, you need a clear head, a steady pulse, and the chance to feel as though you are keeping your head above water. Yet how can we, emotional storytellers that we are, control our emotions enough to enable writing under such trying circumstances?

It's not as difficult as you might think. There are tricks—emotional "hacks," if you will—that can create calm in spite of our haywire psyches. While researching for my book *Facing Every Mom's Fears*, I learned that calm—like fear—has two components: physiological and emotional. Even when emotional calm is out of reach, physiological calm can be nurtured and even *manufactured*. Our physical bodies can be tricked to do an end-run around an emotionally anxious brain. We can deliberately, effectively shift our state of mind to one that is more conducive to writing. Here are some of the best ways to do it.

> # Even when emotional calm is out of reach, physiological calm can be nurtured and even manufactured.

A. Wield the surprising power of scent to shift your mood.

Scent has been proven one of the most powerful emotional triggers. Use that power. Bake something and write while it's in the oven. Buy flowers and set them on your writing desk. Go to the candle store, find something that smells like peace to you, and light it before you sit down to write. If your crisis keeps you away from home, bring the scents of home with you in the form of your favorite shampoo, soap, essential oils, tea, lotion, or candles. Even hospitals will permit soaps from home. The scent might not make you instantly or totally calm, but combined with some other tactics, you may be amazed at scent's ability to calm your spirit and open the door to creativity.

B. Make a soundtrack for peace and productivity.

Technology has made sound more portable and easier than ever. Smartphone apps like Spotify and Pandora allow you to curate a play-anywhere collection of music to suit your needs. Make yourself a writing playlist that feels calm but productive. Or, utilize noise-cancelling headphones if you need silence to make the words come. With repeated use, either strategy will serve as a potent trigger to your muse that "it's time to work" no matter where you are and what you've been doing. Inspirational music, favorite hymns, soft classical guitar, total silence, ocean waves, or even happy pop songs can shift your mood and foster creativity. Simply put, if you can't write inside the world you're in, use sound or silence to make a new one where you *can* write.

> ... if you can't write inside the world you're in, use sound or silence to make a new one where you can write.

C. Get touchy-feely.

Even the youngest infant bears witness to the power of touch. Take care with how you dress during a crisis, ensuring that what touches your skin feels soft and comforting. Ask for and give all the hugs you can stand. Pay attention to the temperature of the room. I believe so powerfully in the healing, comforting power of touch that I launched a prayer shawl ministry at my church. We knit and bless soft, fluffy wraps to give to people in times of crisis. Grab a stuffed animal, pet a cat, snuggle a puppy. Write in a comfy chair instead of your usual desk. If you've never indulged in a massage, now might be an excellent time to start. Any or all of these steps can settle you enough to let the words come out and play.

One of the most absurd-sounding but practical tactics is to put on your pajamas—yes, again with the pajamas. As I mentioned before, most of us naturally associate PJs with calm and comfort. Who cares if it's two p.m.? If you're freaking out, go put on your pajamas. Even just for an hour, or for the thirty minutes you've carved out to write. Your body will physiologically calm down *even if nothing has changed* in your situation. And, it's just silly enough to take the edge off a harrowing day and make a writing sprint possible.

Tactic 5: Build Yourself a Fort of Fours

If any profession is predisposed to "awfulizing"— that talent for taking a situation and dreaming up all the ways it could get worse— it's us writers.

Let's talk about your brain. As a writer, it's your primary work tool. But face it: The vivid imagination that helps you write can be your worst enemy in a crisis. After all, we writers are the what-if experts. If any profession is predisposed to "awfulizing"—that talent for taking a situation and dreaming up all the ways it could get worse—it's us writers. If you're looking for a cooler head to prevail, don't look to a writer. Even so, we writers must take an active role in soothing our minds in times of trouble. My favorite tactic for this is what I call the Fort of Fours. If you journal—and most writers do—this powerful practice will come easily to you. As early in the day as you can manage it, open a journal or notebook. For me, this comes as part of my morning devotional practice. It may come with your morning coffee, right as you wake, or after breakfast. The particulars don't really matter, as long as the practice precedes the start of your active day.

A. List four things for which you are thankful.

Your four things can be big or small, generalized or detailed, long-term or short-term, but they must be *specific to the day*. Gratitude can be harder than you think. I've had days when "the vending machine coffee wasn't nasty" was about the best I could do. It's okay to set a low bar here. The idea is to force yourself to find the good hiding around you amid a bad situation. Doing this first thing in the morning wakes up your optimism's muscles. I know it sounds trite, but anyone who has ever kept a gratitude journal will tell you it works. If you like, wake up your writing brain by describing your four things in great detail. When you look for the good, you will end up finding more of it—even in the darkest of places.

B. List four wishes, prayers, or goals *just for today*.

Even the largest of crises must be handled one day at

a time. Masters of imagination that we are, we writers tend to run ahead of ourselves into tomorrow, next week, or next month to plot potential problems. Planning long-range solutions is useful, but holding all that coping in your head at once isn't likely to help you make it through what you're facing today. Train yourself to walk through a crisis one day at a time. Even if that problem takes years to solve, the one-day-at-a-time mentality will do wonders for your stress level.

> Planning long-range solutions is useful, but holding all that coping in your head at once isn't likely to help you make it through what you're facing today.

You may be in a multi-month search for a new job, but today's task is drafting your résumé. A new diabetes diagnosis presents multiple issues, but today you need to learn how your insulin syringe works. If your car died, step one may be figuring out your budget for a new one. Shave the big issues down into daily goals, and you hand yourself an opportunity for achievement. Simply articulating the four goals is powerful on its own, but if you are a person of prayer, meditation, or visualization, now is the time to bring those practices into play. Woman of faith that I am, I would send up a quartet of highly detailed, specific prayers asking for God's help and provision. A modern version of the classic "give us this day our daily bread."Make these four whatever you want. Draw on your writing skills and describe them in as much detail as you like. Find the perfect verb or imagine how it will feel when it comes to pass. The only rule (and it is rule enough, believe me) is that they must *only* be for the next twenty-four hours. Force that short-term focus into your goals. But be warned: It's often a challenge.

C. Go back and check off the achieved goals or answered prayers or realized wishes from yesterday.

Get ready to be amazed at how many checkmarks find their way into your journal. The accompanying "I did that" or "This came to pass" or "That prayer was answered" is powerful evidence for your own spirit that you can get through whatever you are facing. If it helps, jot down a paragraph about how it felt, what you saw, how those around you responded. Let the writer in you make it as vivid as possible so you can embrace and celebrate the win.

You're a writer, so I know you value writing; but recognize the only hard-and-fast rule of this process: You *must* do this in writing. Seriously, you can't default to just doing this in your head. Why? Because a hard copy list is far more powerful data for your brain than a collection of thoughts. And then you can...

D. Review your long list of checkmarks whenever you need to.

Seven years ago, I started this practice on the suggestion of a friend. I have continued it—in calm times as well as crisis—every day since then. I have pages upon pages of checkmarks to fuel my faith and nurture my optimism. I have scores of written details I can draw on for both emotional support and writing fodder. You can too. Such a small investment reaps huge rewards both as a human being and as a writer seeking to capture and convey deep, truthful emotions.

Each of the tactics shared in this chapter is designed to get you through the thick of a crisis—to keep you afloat as the worst of the storm surrounds you. Steadying your ship is an essential first step for the "how to write" you need. Once you've put these tactics to use, you'll be ready to spur your creative self back into real action. The next chapter will include several practical ways to make that happen.

Chapter 2

Row for Shore: Staying Productive

You may yearn to keep writing. Or, you may have no choice in whether you write. Like everyone else, working writers have had disaster thrust upon them with no regard to their contracts. Either way, you are likely frustrated by how your crisis has stolen your creative energy. You're not alone; it's a particular dilemma for creative people in the middle of trauma to try and gut their way through a project. Nonwriters—or what a colleague jokingly calls "normals"—might not understand how our line of work draws on emotional wells that may have just sprung massive leaks. Other kinds of jobs can hold up more easily under emotional stress, but creating can feel impossible under dire conditions. Still, times arise when there is work that *must* be done, deadlines that *must* be met. Maybe you can't stand how long it's been since you've made any kind of progress. What's a writer to do? Let's explore some tactics specifically designed for restoring, protecting, and rejuvenating your writing muse while you're under fire.

Tactic 1: Inform Your Team... But Do It Wisely

During a crisis, you have a lot of balls in the air at a time when your juggling skills have left the room. How do you ask for help in a way that supports you getting your work done?

A. If you have an agent, confer with him or her *before* contacting your editor.

If you're in a tizzy about meeting your next deadline or handling tomorrow's radio interview without going to pieces, have this conversation with your agent rather than your editor—even if you're on very friendly terms with your editor. Consider letting your agent tackle the challenge of communicating with *anyone* who needs something from you. That layer of protection 1) helps you stay calm, 2) shields you from potential dramatic reactions (valid or otherwise), and 3) keeps you from letting your stress run away with your sense and saying something everyone regrets later.

> Consider letting your agent tackle the challenge of communicating with anyone who needs something from you.

B. If you have an assistant, consider having him or her contact your vendors and publishing partners.

Assistants can offer a layer of protection as well, especially for independently published authors. While self-publishing can offer you much-needed flexibility in times of crisis, it also means the buck stops solely with you. Ask your assistant to help you identify what delays are possible, what consequences an altered timetable might have, and how things can be simplified. That's a lot of communication you may not have energy for at first—with answers that may not induce calm; but having someone else to do this "triage" for you ensures you'll have the information ready without becoming swamped by it while you are still in the first stages of coping.

C. Wait until you can be "informative but not panicky" before calling your editor or other high-stakes partners.

You will earn yourself loads of points for professionalism if you can manage a semblance of grace under pressure. If you have an agent and time is tight, consider having your agent call your editor with the basic urgent details, saying you will touch base as soon as you can. Likewise, your assistant can do this with other partners. What is crucial is that you should not talk with anyone highly impacted by your situation if you still can't keep from crying or getting angry. In the meantime, rely on a cooler head to communicate for you.

> ...you should not talk with anyone highly impacted by your situation if you still can't keep from crying or getting angry.

If you feel you *must* reach out on your own, ask yourself: How will my professional partners respond to a crisis level of emotionality? How significantly will they be impacted by what's happened? Prepare yourself for their responses, remembering that you may be throwing a monster-size wrench into their plans as well. The goal is to ensure that reaching out is a choice *you* make, and at a time of your choosing. Sympathy is always wonderful to receive from colleagues, but strive to keep these conversations as professional as possible.

D. If you are independently published, explore delaying your current or next projects.

Don't let our industry's constant pressure to produce back you into an unnecessary corner. A helpful delay doesn't have to cost you readers or momentum. Unless you are depending on publication income to cover living expenses, remember that *lives are not at stake* in this business. A smartly planned delay isn't likely to end your career, but it may save crucial relationships or even your own health. A note: If you are depending on publishing income to cover life expenses, make plans soon (if you haven't already) to put an emergency fund in place for just such situations.

A smartly planned delay isn't likely to end your career, but it may save crucial relationships or even your own health.

E. Don't ask for a two-week deadline extension when you need six months.

Help your publisher or vendors understand the full weight of the crisis you are facing. Respect the size and the strength of your foe here, and don't confuse denial with courage. Knee-jerk adjustments may feel like progress, but they may end up tying you in tighter knots and raising the very stress levels they were designed to alleviate. Everything from the previous point applies here as well: Delays generally will not kill your career. A good rule of thumb is to take whatever time span feels reasonable *and double it*. You want to overestimate your needs until you have the full scope of the crisis you are facing. If your spouse's car accident injuries are so time-consuming that you are unlikely to make your tight deadline, own up to it *now*—not two weeks before the book is due. If your grandchildren are coming to live with you for six weeks, acknowledge *now* what that chaos will do to your daily word count for a while. Once the project is done, your editors, coworkers, or collaborators will be thankful that you gave yourself a wide, workable margin instead of read-justing to a second or third missed deadline.

Tactic 2: Look for New Ways to Get Work Done

When you're faced with a crisis, getting the words down on the page can seem an impossible task. Your deadline doesn't really care about your current blood pressure level, and sometimes the job simply *must get done*. But how to coax those words out? This is the most daunting challenge facing creative professionals, to be sure. I polled a variety of working writers who met deadlines under a number of traumatic situations. They shared the following list of tips.

A. Try small batches in new formats.

Write 250 words—the equivalent of a page—and see how it feels. Does the escape into your writing serve as a relief? Even if it feels hugely difficult, give yourself at least a handful of tries at productivity. The trick is to pick a word count that feels doable—even if it must be tiny. One hundred words, for example, can fit on an index card. I suspect even the most traumatized of writers could manage four imperfect sentences that can be edited later. Can you tuck three or four index cards into your pocket and set yourself the challenge of filling them? Dictate into the voice memo function of your smartphone? Write one page in a small notebook? Find whatever helps to make a small chunk of writing feel manageable. All you need at first—maybe all you need *at all*—are baby steps.

B. If you feel you can't escape your situation, start by describing it.

Many books—fiction and nonfiction—have been born of personal difficulties (more on that in Chapter 4). Writing about where you are right now can "prime the pump," proving to your creative self that writing is possible. Remember those descriptions from your Fort of Fours? Your lists and descriptions may give you the strength and encouragement you need to segue back to your original project. As a bonus, you may also discover the seeds of a new project in the process.

C. Change locations.

Chemo involves a lot of waiting, and patients often

sleep. A laptop and a highly transportable muse made writing in the hospital room or chemo suite possible for me. You may discover, however, that you need to give yourself time in a different location in order to compartmentalize your brain space. Ritualize it if it helps, saying: "At two p.m. I walk across the street to get my cup of coffee and do my writing," or "When I get home I make myself a cup of tea and write." Remind yourself this is your time to work, and when you return home, go to the hospital, or head to wherever this crisis is currently set, you can be fully present knowing you've done your needed work.

D. Don't feel guilty if you crave the escape writing offers.

One writer I know was surprised to discover that trauma shut down her internal editor and allowed words to gush out. She didn't have time or energy to strive for excellence, so she let go of her expectations and just kept typing. She craved the escape and the feeling of productivity, and she needed a visit to the world of her book where she was in charge. At the time, she didn't have the strength to care about quality. But when she returned to the work to revise, she discovered her work had an urgency and clarity she'd not found before. Progress happened for her, and it can happen for you. Embrace that for the gift it is. Take care not to ignore your crisis when it needs your attention, but remind yourself and others that it is okay to work if it helps you cope.

E. Compartmentalize your muse—or your biz.

...while some parts of your writing feel beyond your grasp, not *all* parts will elude you, even in the worst of moments.

As writers, different parts of our creativity tackle different tasks. You may love the alchemy of writing a first draft, but editing and revising make you twitch. You may find social media fun and engaging, while filling a blank page feels like torture. Not all of what we do comes from the same well of creativity. This can mean that while some parts of your writing feel beyond your grasp, not *all* parts will elude you, even in the worst of moments. With a little bit of experimentation, you will discover which parts of your crisis stymie which parts of your muse. In my case, I could edit or proofread just about anywhere, but under pressure I had tremendous difficulty writing a first draft. One writer discovered that the business side of independent publishing came easier to her in a crisis, even though drafting felt beyond her. Conversely, another writer found the first draft offered a blessed escape from his stress, while any promotional tasks or edits felt impossible. Categorize your current workload and sort the pieces by how easy they are. Start with the tasks that are easiest until you feel ready to tackle the hard ones. Or simply keep to the easy tasks until things let up a bit and give you energy for the hard ones. Doing so not only gives you better planning information, but also may reveal some useful coping mechanisms. You may discover that your unfinished manuscript may be as much an ally as an albatross.

F. Check for obstacles.

If you are the patient, are any of the treatments you are currently undergoing known for sapping energy, concentration, or clarity? Beta-blockers, thyroid meds, and other prescriptions are well-known for messing with mood and creative energy. When my migraines increased again a few years ago, my doctor described a common preventative drug to reduce their frequency. Though successfully tolerated by other patients, the drug's side effects of low-level dizziness and minor fuzziness of thought were completely intolerable to me. I found I could not speak publicly or write while even the slightest bit dizzy or foggy. We scratched that option off my list and went in search of better alternatives. Check with your doctor to see which options will best suit the specific needs of our profession. If your doctor doesn't understand your unique needs, go find one that does.

G. Embrace the lousy first draft.

Brilliance is likely beyond your reach—even if you discover you work great under pressure. Tell yourself: "It doesn't have to be perfect; it just has to be written." You can revise and polish your draft at another time once you get through the difficult stage of putting the words down on paper no matter how inelegant they feel. As best-selling author Nora Roberts famously said, "You can't fix a blank page."

H. Set a timer.

Pick whatever span of time feels possible—even fifteen minutes. Most of us can stand fifteen minutes of almost anything. Once or twice a day, set the timer and have at it. During those minutes, give yourself permission to "be a writer" rather than someone ill, caring, or coping. Starting is often the hardest part, and you may discover you can work longer than you think.

> During those minutes, give yourself permission to "be a writer" rather than someone ill, caring, or coping.

I. Outline in more detail than you normally do.

Knowing exactly what happens next can help lure you to the keyboard. Even if it focuses your writing more on the plot, remember you can layer in the emotion at another time. Take your synopsis and break it down into chapters. Then break the chapters down into scenes or sections. Keep adding levels of detail until you can see a comfortable road map of what you need to do next. Then pick a portion that feels possible and do it.

J. Go through the motions.

One writer started her day by typing an existing newsletter article or magazine story in order to get her fingers typing. Eventually, the muscle memory would jump-start her writing brain, and a bit of story would emerge. Type a segment of a favorite book, since nothing gets a writer's creative juices flowing like great writing. Let you fingers inspire your mind as you type great words.

K. Try dictation.

Chances are you won't need any special equipment for dictation because most computers and nearly every smartphone comes preloaded with some form of basic dictation software. If typing feels beyond you—or if you have a physical limitation such as carpal tunnel syndrome, eyesight issues, a bad back, or a broken wrist—close your eyes and dictate a scene, a setting, or even a character description to get you started. Carry on dictating as long as you can. An added benefit of dictation: You can't edit or see mistakes, so there's nothing to impede your progress.

L. Pull an all-nighter.

Some of us would be a wreck before two a.m., but others got through college this way. If you used to have the all-nighter in your toolbox, now might be the time to resurrect it—because you're probably not sleeping well anyway. Be *very careful* and very sparing, however, in how you implement this. Lack of sleep can launch a host of its own problems.

Tactic 3: Wave a White Flag
(Yes, Surrender Is an Option)

Despite the title of this book, it would be irresponsible of me to skip the tactic of surrendering to your circumstances. "Never give up, never give in" can be a dangerous choice, and stopping writing is usually an option. We are all far more than the sum of our occupations, and there are times when lives *really are* at stake. One colleague of mine is fond of saying, "Your books will never come visit you in the nursing home." While it may feel like a drastic last option, remember that you can survive postponing or walking away from work.

As you make your way through an ordeal, continually evaluate whether or not it is wise to continue writing. Make that choice before the choice forces itself upon you in the form of a physical, emotional, or financial crisis.

Make that choice before the choice forces itself upon you in the form of a physical, emotional, or financial crisis.

After pushing on toward a deadline, one writer stopped altogether when she knew her father was in his last days. Though there was some professional fallout from her decision, she does not regret that choice. And, it's important to note, she has continued with her career. Some things really *are* more important than your deadline.

One of those things may be your own health. While I like to think we did a good job managing the challenges of my son's illness, at a point the stress finally took its toll on my own health. Three months into the chemotherapy treatments, I woke up one morning without the ability to absorb new or recent information. Roughly four days of my life went missing, and I have almost no recollection of the actual episode except what others have told me. According to my doctors, I experienced "transient global amnesia." Go ahead and make the romance novel amnesia jokes—I've heard them all. I knew basic context, but not recent changes. I knew my identity, my family, my home—but not that my daughter was at summer camp, how my son got the gadget he was holding, or what year it was. A human "unable to save; disk is full." It's a sad commentary on our lives at that point that my son knew exactly how to calmly call the paramedics, and I was rushed to the hospital under suspicion that the stress of his illness had caused me to have a stroke.

Talk about taking a bad situation and making it a thousand times worse! Thankfully, it was not a stroke; transient global amnesia is a rare vascular phenomenon that happens most frequently to migraine patients. Though no exact cause for transient global amnesia is known, it didn't take a neurosurgeon's expertise to view this as a wake-up call for my stress level. Even though I was on track for an adjusted contract deadline, my agent gave me a straightforward "halt work" command, and I obeyed it. For the next three months, I dropped all writing and concentrated on getting all of us through the last of my son's treatments in the best possible physical and emotional health. My career survived, my son survived, the episode has not reoccurred in the seven years since, and it is likely to never occur again. We have almost arrived at the point where my amnesia episode is an odd and amusing sidebar to a difficult season of our lives.

Resilience is a noble quality, but there may come a time where it is a better choice to face a hard truth: You may not be able to write through everything. You should not be expected to write through everything. So yes, you can surrender. You can stop writing. That doesn't make you a bad writer; it means you are a good human being.

> You may not be able to write
> through everything. You
> should not be expected to
> write through everything.

We have focused our attention on your individual coping with crises. Let us shift our attention to the world around us. We wade through a crisis with others beside us—and that can be as much a hindrance as a help. And, let's face it: The introverted nature of most writers makes communication and relationships challenging on a good day. To help with that, the next chapter will address how to communicate with family, friends, associates, and our audiences in ways that make room for connection while respecting and protecting your right to personal privacy.

Chapter 3

Raise a Flag: Who Hears What, and When?

Crises don't happen in a vacuum. For better or worse, they happen in community. They erupt alongside people we love and associates who irritate us. We deal with emergencies in front of our dearest friends as well as the grocery checkout clerk. How you, individually, handle your crisis is only a portion of the picture. Every writer needs tactics for communicating with family, friends, coworkers, and others.

...find a way to let a support system into your life without letting well-meaning meddlers take over.

Like most writers, you may be a raging introvert. You think you'd cope so much better if the world would just leave you alone—which is unlikely to happen. Yet study after study has confirmed the vital role of community and connection in healing. You increase your chances of locating sanity and productivity if you can find a way to let a support system into your life without letting well-meaning meddlers take over.

If you are a published author or a successful columnist, blogger, or speaker, you also have a public to manage. It is wise to deal with that dynamic proactively, not reactively, because public information can be an uncontrollable beast, and you don't need any more stress. In this chapter, we'll take a look at the various levels of connection—from those who know you well to your (hopefully) adoring public—and review strategies for handling them.

Tactic 1: Draw Strength from Your Inner Circle

Your closest friends, immediate family, partners, and spouses will likely be nearby when crisis hits. And that's a good thing. Gather them. You need them. They want to be there for you. But they likely will bring their own issues and stresses. Remember these steps when dealing with those closest to you.

A. Agree to give your loved ones the unedited version.

Enter into an up-front agreement with your inner circle that now is no time to filter your words. Ask them for the grace of unedited communication, even when it might feel inappropriate. They will likely understand that you need to spend your energies elsewhere. If you need to vent—or cry or yell or make terrible jokes—these are the folks to call.

B. Don't assume this role belongs to your family.

Your inner circle needs to be comprised of people who can be agents of calm. Those people aren't always family members. Anyone with a gift for drama—and every family's got 'em—isn't a good choice for your inner circle.

> Your inner circle needs to be comprised of people who can be agents of calm.

C. Don't forget to consider crisis and care professionals.

Nurses, counselors, outplacement professionals, and financial planners can all be effective members of your inner circle. Experience and objectivity can lend a hand, even if it's a hired hand. When my mother died unexpectedly, one of the most surprising members of my inner circle turned out to be her stockbroker—someone I'd never even met before that time. Building your core team isn't solely about logic or even function; it's about trust and chemistry. If you connect with someone, don't hesitate to pull them into your inner circle.

Tactic 2: Widen Your Scope to an Outer Circle

As writers, we are beings of communication. Whether we are introverts or extroverts, we are still natural storytellers, likely to process our lives in narrative form. This tendency may mean we tell everyone too much of what's going on, or that we stuff everything inside until we can write it down in the hopes of making sense of it. Either tendency makes it wise to think about how we communicate to the rest of our world, the realms of influence and interaction beyond our inner circle. Take time to think about contact with this wider circle so you don't fall prey to knee-jerk instincts in the heat of a dilemma.

I'm an extrovert, which means I *need* to tell the story—pretty much to anyone who will listen. Emotionally, with far too much detail, and multiple times...you get the picture. If you are the opposite, however, this can pose a different difficulty because some people outside your inner circle really do need to know what's going on in your life and want to help. Consider the following guidelines to decipher how to inform colleagues, associates, and acquaintances about your current predicament.

A. Give appropriate and edited details.

Take a few moments to craft a short version of what has happened. Tap into your skills by writing it down and editing it several times for brevity and clarity. What you want is an "elevator speech": a thirty-second version of your situation. Three sentences, tops—one or two if you can manage it. Choose which details the world can know and which are best kept only for those closest to you. If your parent is suffering from dementia, do you want the whole world to hear about the latest lapse that landed you both in the emergency room? While it's tempting to defend yourself from a scathing review or a dropped contract, you don't want to give any rejection too much airtime. Your latest financial hit isn't everyone's business, nor is the state of your health or marriage. Some jobs end in more dignified ways than others—so can you craft a professional statement to communicate you are now looking for new employment without trash-talking the boss who just sacked you? A good, tight script at the ready means you are less likely to flood someone with too many details or miss a chance to appropriately gain an associate's wisdom or assistance.

> What you want is an "elevator speech": a thirty-second version of your situation.

B. Keep an eye out for new allies.

One of the great gifts of a traumatic situation is that it can connect you deeply with people you previously considered only casual acquaintances. You may discover your pharmacist once survived a serious car accident. A neighbor just lost a beloved pet as well. A coworker may have never mentioned losing their house to a fire. Discovering people around you who've had a similar experience brings a gift of commonality. You help yourself by communicating enough information to let surprising new resources come your way.

C. Edit if you are an extrovert; proclaim if you are an introvert.

We extroverted storytellers need to tell the story—it's part of our coping process—but we likely need to edit the story first. Contemplating how to communicate with your outer circle helps you meet that need without "oversharing"—which extroverts can fall prey to under stress. On the other hand, introverted storytellers might need some introspection to decide *who* should know *what*. Remember, introverts, that the circle may need to be larger than you find comfortable at first. Most importantly, recognize that there may be true benefits to widening the pool of those who know what you're facing.

...there may be true benefits to widening the pool of those who know what you're facing.

Tactic 3: Craft a Strategy for "Everybody Else"

If you are published, or in any other way a public figure, you have a third dynamic to manage: everybody else. How will your audience, your readers, your employees, and even the general public hear what's happened? What information do they need and deserve? Should they simply be asked to respect your privacy? These are smart questions to consider when trauma hits.

The decision may not be yours alone. When my son's illness became serious enough to halt some of my professional work, we had a frank conversation about how and when to let the world know. I asked him specifically what details he felt it was okay for the world to know and which he deemed private. Person of faith that I am, I welcomed the prayers and good wishes of my readers, and I felt obligated to let them know why I "disappeared" for a while. The internet and reality television have birthed a public all too hungry for the gory details—so much so that speculation has the potential to create tales far different or worse than the truth.

You may not need to go so far as to issue a press release or statement, but if you do, choose a representative to deliver this for you if you feel it requires a live delivery rather than a written distribution. Do not place yourself in the position of taking questions until you are absolutely ready. Reporters aren't known for their restraint or compassion amid such circumstances.

When preparing to deal with the general public—such as strangers, your readers, or the press—keep the following in mind.

A. Script your communication.

Even if you are an excellent speaker, you are not at your best right now. Write out what you want to say and consider the best way to say it. Even if you don't opt for reading or memorizing your statement, the scripting process itself will put the right language in your head.

B. Design a short script that will end the conversation.

Remember the elevator speech? Come up with a one-sentence version of your situation *that doesn't invite questions*. When a project I loved dearly crashed and burned, readying the phrase "It wasn't received as well as I'd hoped" kept me from gushing all the horrid details of that failure and kept the conversation moving forward. Brevity is especially useful if you've been fired, sued, or wronged in any other personal or professional manner. In these situations, the temptation to air your grievances can be recklessly strong. Craft short, passive voice sentences, such as: "My marriage has come to an end" or "A loss has occurred in my family."

C. Decide whose privacy is at stake.

Traumas are rarely solo acts. Take some time to decide how the involved parties need their privacy protected. If your mom is in her final days, does the world need to know details? Or can you simply say you're helping a member of your family through a medical crisis? Does the world need to know your son failed out of school? If your problem stems from you needing to manage another's crisis, ask them directly what they feel comfortable sharing and find an appropriate boundary together. If you are in the hot seat, take a breath and ask yourself how much detail is too much. Perhaps talk this through with a good friend. An ounce of forethought can prevent you from spilling something that was better left unsaid.

...ask yourself how much
detail is too much.

D. Decide what is gained by everyone knowing.

You may find the answer to be a profound motivator. Or the answer may be "nothing." We've become a society of oversharers who know far too much about the personal lives of our celebrities, politicians, sports stars, etc.; but sometimes our information can empower people who are going through similar struggles. Michael J. Fox made huge strides for Parkinson's disease by going public with his medical challenges. Mothers Against Drunk Driving was founded by a woman determined to use her devastating loss to raise awareness and save future lives. These are powerful reasons to go public. Other celebrities, however, have given us so many details about their latest traumas that we shift from commiseration to outright annoyance.

Tactic 4: Consider Taking It Public

There are many reasons to be forthcoming about whatever you are facing. Most of us want to find purpose in our pain, and helping or informing others is one of the strongest ways to do that. If you are an extrovert, or if you have a speaking career, going public may feel like the whole point of whatever has happened to you. Here are some compelling reasons to take your story to an audience.

A. Others can learn from you.

Many a public announcement regarding disease or tragedy has begun with the statement, "If I can save one life..." or "If I can keep one family from having to go through what we're going through..." We yearn for some good to come out of our current overdose of bad. No one can speak to the healing power of forgiveness like one who has been grievously wronged. It's likely others in your situation will be encouraged and strengthened by whatever message you can deliver in person or through your writing. Tremendous satisfaction and grace—especially if you are a person of faith—can come from using your writing talent to make the world a better place. Having something positive to offer the world can prevent you from feeling like a powerless victim amid bad circumstances.

B. People may (eventually) hear about it anyway.

If you have to cancel public appearances, miss book deadlines, delay releases, or take a social media break, the public will likely know something is up. You simply won't be as focused or dependable as you normally are, and that can risk leaving a bad impression. Sympathy for your difficult position is far preferable to speculation about why you have been dropping the ball. Remember in 2012 when late-night television host Stephen Colbert disappeared off the air for a week without warning? Speculation went wild until it was announced that the star's mother was gravely ill. Then, Colbert experienced a huge outpouring of compassion and support. If you know your public or professional functions will be affected, it might be the best choice for everyone to know at least part of the reason—unless, of course, privacy dictates silence. The media—or even just the town gossip mill—abhors a vacuum, and people will try to fill it whether you like it or not. You don't have to spill everything (unless you want to), but with a little forethought, you can fill that vacuum on your own terms. The narrative *you* control is always a better choice than the one others create for you.

> The narrative you control is always a better choice than the one others create for you.

C. It takes less energy to be transparent.

Telling the truth always takes less energy than anything else. Keeping secrets—even appropriate ones—takes energy. If you are facing a medical challenge, you may find tremendous support awaiting you when you go public. Might it be best to focus your energy on healing or your treatment rather than a cover-up of evidence or symptoms? If your marriage has ended, are you better off making excuses for a missing partner or finding an appropriate way to disclose the situation so everyone can move on? And let's face it: It's much harder to find a new publisher or agent if no one realizes you're looking.

I'm not suggesting you splay your soul open to the world—television and the internet have plenty of people far too eager to do that—but thoughtfully consider what it is costing you to "keep up appearances" that may not need keeping up.

Tactic 5: Consider Keeping It Private

Let us take a look at the other side of the coin. Why should you avoid going public with your crisis? While opting for transparency has its benefits, there are some very good reasons why you may choose to keep your situation to yourself.

A. You may not be prepared for negative outcomes.

People can be tactless, nosy, and even cruel. Not everyone will respond with kindness and compassion. Inevitably some people will become accusatory or combative out of their own fear, emotional baggage, discomfort, ignorance, or thoughtlessness. You may get questions that push for far more than you are ready to share. And you will most likely get a barrage of advice—not all of it good or useful.

Whether it makes sense or not, and whether they have the whole story or not, people can be remarkably unkind. When my son was sick, I heard things that made me shake my head and want to say, "You didn't just say that. You *couldn't have* meant that the way it sounded." Some of the proposed theories for how my son got cancer made me want to go home and cry for hours. In my experience, the good far outweighed the bad, but the bad really stung. If you aren't yet strong enough for it, it may be a better choice to keep the situation private.

B. You don't owe anyone an explanation.

You don't. "It's personal" is a complete sentence, and it's all the explanation you need. If you violate a contract or employment issues are involved, then some form of explanation to certain people may be required. The truth is, most people don't need or want the full details. Even for your closest circle, "I'm going through a difficult time right now" is a perfectly acceptable response. If someone presses, a firm "I'd rather not talk about it" can be useful. Your personal business is just that—personal.

> # "It's personal" is a complete sentence, and it's all the explanation you need.

C. Your energy may be required elsewhere.

Though it takes energy to keep something private, it takes energy when something goes public as well. Anyone who has had to answer a surge of texts, Facebook comments, or emails from concerned friends and fans will tell you it takes effort to give everyone an explanation or update. Having to relay the same difficult information over and over also takes an emotional toll. Sharing sites like CaringBridge have made medical traumas easier to share, but not every situation fits into a blog or a Facebook page. A hairstylist friend of mine who was widowed suddenly and early in life said one of the most difficult parts of returning to work was having to recount her story over and over to each of her clients. If your beloved science fiction series has failed, it's disheartening to explain it to twelve different people a day. Yes, you may very well receive compassion in return, but that may not entirely balance the cost of reliving your situation.

D. You've chosen your career; your family has not.

You want to be a writer. You want readers and fans. You love having people who share your stories and who want to hear more of your gifts. You have chosen the relationship with your readers. Your family? Not so much. If you share with your readership that your father is in his last days, you bring him into the spotlight right alongside you. Consider that dynamic. Some traumas only involve us, but many involve friends, family, neighbors, or employers. Do you have the right to shine a public light on their circumstance? Be sure to take their wishes and feelings into account.

As I said, my son and I had many conversations about how and what to tell my readers about his illnesses. We turned down some interviews—despite the extraordinary nature of his story and the wonderful outcome of his recovery—because he simply didn't want to do them. I am permitted to share some aspects of our experience and not others, and it is his decision alone where that line falls. Take the time to talk to those involved. You don't want whatever crisis you are facing now to be compounded by relationship damage that may never heal.

You don't want whatever crisis you are facing now to be compounded by relationship damage that may never heal.

Tactic 6: Consider Giving It More Thought

If you have weighed the pros and cons of going public with your situation, here are some additional thoughts to consider before moving forward.

A. Communication started can't be stopped.

You will not be able to change your mind once you have revealed the information. It will be out there—permanently. That's not always a reason to fear, but it is a reason to stop and think. If you are a person of faith, you may be hearing a clear message in prayer that lets you know you can handle whatever comes next. Even if you are not, your personal convictions may clearly tell you it's time to share your experience with the world. That's a fine thing, and many people will likely benefit from your courage. Just make sure you understand the irrevocable nature of what you are doing.

> ...make sure you understand the irrevocable nature of what you are doing.

B. It may be too soon.

You may be sure that going public is the right thing to do, but it may be too soon. Can you talk about it without crying uncontrollably? I think it's perfectly fine to cry in speeches or interviews—I've done it countless times—as long as it does not prevent you from continuing. We've all seen someone unable to go on because they are overwhelmed, and their emotions can be the most moving part of a funeral or other remembrance. But such an overwhelming moment has its place, and it isn't everywhere. If the wounds are too fresh for you to withstand challenges or attacks, consider waiting until more healing has taken place.

C. You may lack the necessary grace to cut someone slack.

Inevitably, you will have to cut someone slack for a thoughtless remark or show grace when someone attacks. It will happen. When confronted with some of life's messier elements, people say dumb and hurtful things whether they mean to or not. Such people are tough enough to handle in a private setting, but they demand an extra supply of grace and tact in public. If you don't yet have the emotional stability to not rise to someone's bait, consider waiting. If you fly off the handle in a public setting because of an accusation or inconsiderate comment, the resulting damage could make a current crisis much worse.

If you expect your public or private sharing to produce only compassion and support, you will be disappointed—maybe even from the last person you'd expect. Someone in my community—we'll call her Mom X—was actually upset with me that her son was told my son had cancer. Mom X felt it was disturbing information for a thirteen-year-old to hear. She preferred the school to tell students he was "sick" rather than use "that scary *cancer* word."

I was appalled for months, until I realized she was simply frightened. She feared her son couldn't handle an up close exposure to childhood cancer. Fear makes us say thoughtless things. We all have been guilty of being too scared to think with compassion.

My realization, however, doesn't change the fact that the day Mom X called to share her thoughts, I cried for an hour in the privacy of my own home. I am very glad we waited another two months to tell my readership my son had cancer. By then, my feet were more solidly beneath me, and I could better deal with the dings and stabs I knew were coming. Perhaps you might need to do the same.

You do yourself and those you love a true favor if you thoughtfully consider how the world hears of your situation. Life blindsides us. When emotions run high, you may not get to ponder any of these things. Mistakes, poor choices, and lashing out can't be totally avoided, so don't dwell on your lapses. Instead, take every chance you can to utilize wise communication strategies. They will buy you peace and progress as you face what's ahead.

Chapter 4

Fill Your Sail: Writing About Your Experience

As writers, life is our material. We yearn to know how, when, and why to use our sorrowful or challenging experiences in our work.

The problem is, we can rarely be wise about experiences while in the thick of them. Everything feels important, and we make assumptions or jump to conclusions for the sake of control or closure. Our emotions run high, which can't be changed; it's part of what makes us writers. Besides, shutting ourselves off from the high potency of current experiences is harmful to ourselves and others. We *need* to fully experience what's happening to us right now.

But we also need time. And while taking such time is hard, I believe it is *essential* when preparing to write or speak. You may want to process the current challenge right away using the written word; it's how we think as writers, after all. If you are filling your journal rapidly, good for you. It means you are taking all that is happening in your life and trying to make sense of it. But when is it time to take it beyond your own journal and into the pages of a book, article, blog, or other media?

Tactic 1: Take the Time to Know What Matters

The trouble with us writers and speakers is that we want to make sense of it all *right now*, before we have gained the perspective we may need, or before we know what truly matters. Things that seem trivial now may prove highly important months or years from now. Conversely, things that seemed dire in the middle of a crisis may end up being so trivial we wonder why we ever worried about them. For good reason, the standard advice given to a grieving spouse is not to make major decisions for at least one year. We need that time to process, to acquire some distance, and to let the emotionality of the crisis die down a bit so we can think more clearly.

Bluntly put, if you shouldn't sell your house four months after losing your spouse, you probably shouldn't write a book about it either.

Think of it like parenting. I remember being wildly upset at my daughter's first D in the fifth grade. Actually, it may have been an F, but the fact that I can't remember should tell you something. It had been a difficult year, and this lapse was my daughter's first big academic slipup. I cried. I actually called the principal because this was one of many issues with a problematic teacher. I called my mother-in-law for advice because she was a fourth-grade teacher.

> ...if you shouldn't sell your house four months after losing your spouse, you probably shouldn't write a book about it either.

You could say I overreacted—and you'd be right. I cringe and laugh about this now that my daughter has graduated college and is on her own, making a successful, independent life in her mid-twenties. That fifth-grade D wasn't nearly the crisis it seemed, but I didn't know it at the time. I didn't have the perspective because I was too close to the situation.

On the other hand, I can think of several issues I brushed off as minor, only to discover their significance one or two years later. So often *we just don't know what matters*. We don't know we've made mistakes until they come back around to haunt us. We can't see many of our successes because fruition happens months or even years down the road. The children's hospital that treated my son asks parents to wait a full year before returning as volunteers. I can see why; you can't truly help—no matter how much you may want to—if you're still on the road to recovery yourself.

As I mentioned earlier, I wrote a parenting book called *Facing Every Mom's Fears* while my kids were still young. So many things change quickly as we parent, but I was sure I had gained perspective on things fast enough to write about the challenge of mothering in a frightening world. In today's near-instant electronic publishing market, I might have rushed that manuscript to print in my desire to reach moms who, like me, had been deeply rattled by the events of September 11, 2001. The long process to write and then edit that book (it released in 2004) became important—essential, even—as I processed the many experiences I included from my own life and the lives of other moms around me.

One experience was a huge fight between my own mother and me. The details don't really matter here, but it was a doozy—the kind that iced our relationship for months afterward. It was fourteen years behind me at the time of *Facing Every Mom's Fears*, but I had only recently come to understand her viewpoint. And I don't think I could have written that passage with any authenticity even one year before. Some realizations only come with time, no matter how much we want to rush insight to the table.

> Some realizations only come with time, no matter how much we want to rush insight to the table.

I'm not saying you have to wait fourteen years to write about whatever is burning in your heart lately. You may only have to wait a little while to write what matters. I will recommend this one thing: Resist sharing until you know what matters. Journal all you want, draft as much as you can stand, but don't take your work out into the world until you can sift out the important and universal lesson. What matters, what became important, what proved to stay with you long beyond the crisis—these are the lessons you can give to the world, the teaching points that will make your story valuable.

If you're an extrovert like me, you will want to rush this. You want to bring the world into your situation because connecting with people brings you energy. We covered some of this ground on communication in Chapter 3. I've caught myself rushing to speak on several subjects because I'm convinced the ability to teach others will give the pain value.

We'll cover speaking in the next chapter—for the many of us who speak as well as write—but it's true for writing as well. My urge to validate my pain doesn't mean I have the proper viewpoint yet to help someone else.

> When I write about something, I want to strive for significance. Don't you?

Indeed, one of the most vivid examples of this does come from the speaking world. Someone stands at the podium, often crying, speaking passionately about an experience—but as you look at them, you can tell it's *all about them*. I call it "The Public Wail." News accounts are full of them. Reality television thrives on them. Such displays can spur compassion, disdain, or any number of emotions, but they rarely teach. They rarely serve. That's because they don't connect with us on anything but an emotional level—and no writer wants that for their work. When you can share the emotion but also share what matters about an issue, your work takes on a new significance. When I write about something, I want to strive for significance. Don't you?

It's hard to wait until you know what matters. Holding off until you have unearthed the lesson that is meant to be shared with others requires determination. The rewards are great, however, if you achieve that level of perspective before you take your message out into the world.

Tactic 2: Dig Until You Discover the Universal Truth

Your story means a great deal to you, and it likely means a great deal to those around you. They have watched you struggle with your challenge, supported you when it got bad, and cheered for you when the victories came.

These things are wonderful. That's the best part of life and community—experiencing the support, encouragement, and sympathy of those around you. Your story matters even more to them because they've been part of it.

When you're pondering whether to go public with your adversity, you may assume that the whole world will react the same way. After all, your pain is so very real to you; surely it will ring true for others. I'm not saying that it won't—it very likely will—but you have to put some thought into your message first.

Let me introduce you to a concept I call the Universal Truth. Simply put, the Universal Truth is the "what matters" we're seeking in Tactic 1. It is the heart of your story that goes further than you, the lesson that goes beyond circumstance or personality or details. The Universal Truth is the essence of your story that will resonate not only with those who know you, but also with others in similar or even different situations. It's the lessons you learned, the strengths you acquired, and the things that didn't kill you but made you stronger.

Let's use the supreme challenge of elder-care as example. Many of us find ourselves in this boat or on the brink of boarding. The experience will be different for every person because the details and personalities vary greatly, but what are some of the universal truths in play here? Here are some takeaways I'd list.

Universal Truth example 1: Self-care isn't selfish; it's survival.

Elder-care—any long-term caretaking, actually—is exhausting. Any caretaker not continually watching out for their own health and well-being can get sucked dry. Will an onslaught of demands take your character to her breaking point? Can you convey a list of self-care suggestions in your nonfiction book or article? Think about how to convey this important truth to your readers either in story or instruction.

Universal Truth example 2: Elder-care isn't linear.

Many crises become a roller coaster of setbacks and progression, but elder-care offers some of the fastest turns—often in a one-two punch of whiplash proportions. Just when your fictional heroine thinks she's found the solution to problem A, give her a plot twist where problem B dumps a whole new set of challenges that force her to open up to your hero. Come alongside your nonfiction reader's frustrations and offer ways to cope with the unpredictable nature of their challenge.

Universal Truth example 3: Patience and kindness are decisions, not reactions.

The strongest protagonist can win readers' hearts by

managing to stay soft. You'll find no shortage of plot conflict here; people in pain or fear rarely behave well, especially to those closest to them. How can you show your characters choosing to treat a difficult person with kindness and empathy? How can you help your nonfiction readers develop the nerves of steel and iron will required to stay compassionate?

Points like these make the difference between a book describing elder-care and a meaningful story that reaches and teaches those in the elder-care trenches. Absolutely recount details and stories to bring the experience alive and help the reader "live" in the world you've seen. Make sure, however, that you also put in the time and thought to identify the vital lessons worth passing on—otherwise, you'll only have told a story.

I believe identifying the Universal Truth helps you avoid the trap of "here's what you should do" recommendations. What worked for you may not work for everyone. How I handled the endless stream of surprise crises that came with my aging parents may be the worst tactic for someone else. By digging deep through your experiences to harvest the large and powerful lessons, you push past "do this" and move to the deeper waters of "here's what I learned that I think is true for everyone."

Tactic 3: Choose Close but Not Identical Stories When Writing Fiction

I absolutely believe you can write fiction based on your personal experience. In fact, I think such stories can be among the most powerful fiction of all. But fictionalizing your experience will require some thought before you move forward.

Perhaps your personal life is the last thing you want to write about. In that case, fiction can provide a welcome contrast. One writer I know was facing the terminal illness of her mother. As a romance author, the love and light and happy endings of her work had to go up a notch because the work became her escape. The bliss on the page became her best defense against the angst in the rest of her world.

My experience was different. The first novel I attempted after my son's illness couldn't help but be about a mother protecting a son in danger. My life was too full of all those emotions; it was inevitably going to show up in my work. I knew exactly how it felt, I knew the gut-wrenching progression of events, and it felt *so cathartic* to get it out on the page. I was rewriting my life at a time when I could sure use a do-over. After all, don't they say, "Write what you know"?

My editor was smart enough to realize the dynamic in play, and we worked to come up with the smartest possible tactic to proceed: close but not identical. Yes, real life makes for the seeds of good fiction, but it often doesn't make for good fiction alone. Before you set yourself up for needing to alter details of a highly transformative, real-life experience to serve a fictional plot, consider writing something similar rather than something identical. This is fiction, after all. Besides, would you really want to put yourself into a situation where any negative review of the story or character could feel like a jab at your personal life?

I spent some time identifying the Universal Emotional Truth of my family's remission experience. It wasn't hard to figure out that the primary emotion of that time was fear—more specifically, fear for my son's healthy survival, and fear that the ravages of his illness wouldn't ever fully leave his body or his spirit. I mourned that—at the tender age of thirteen—his future would always include the words *cancer survivor* and *remission*.

> ...consider writing something similar rather than something identical.

Writing about a mother in that exact circumstance would have presented a minefield of writing traps because *I lacked all objectivity*. I would have taken every criticism—even a lukewarm review—highly personal. Instead, I was wisest to find something similar, a situation with the same emotional truth, so that I could draw on my own experience without getting bogged down by it. I chose to write *Falling for the Fireman*, a story about a single mother guiding her son through the survival of a fire that destroyed their family home. Her fears for her middle school son reflected my own: Would the emotional trauma of the disaster ever fully leave him? Could he rebuild after the complete loss of his belongings?

The strategy worked—but not at first. My research gave me great data about how fire affects teens, as well as the path to teenage arson and the many amazing recovery programs that help troubled young fire victims. I had scores of details with astounding correlations to childhood illnesses.

I also had a wildly angsty first draft.

And second draft.

In fact, it took *four revisions* to tone that book down to a place where it didn't feel like an emotional shotgun going off on every page. This is the strongest possible case I can make for *never attempting such work without an editor.* Ever. Even with the margin of "close but not identical," I had lost the ability to balance the emotional narrative of the book. I am convinced that had I attempted a "cancer mom" book, even six rewrites couldn't have brought it around. A cancer book might not have been possible at all, and I'm glad I never tried.

Think of it like a Venn diagram. There's an intersection of truth that your experience shares with everyone:

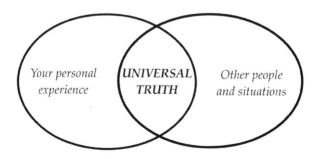

Now, if I were to make another chart applying that Universal Emotional Truth to the novel I just described, it would look like this:

Draw your own diagrams to explore your experience and how it might show up in a work of fiction. What's the Universal Emotional Truth of your experience? Can you devise a plot where that Universal Emotional Truth also appears? Might it be wiser to use that for your story instead of mining your own life too directly?

I'm not advocating keeping your life off the page. Every good author knows some of yourself must go into every work for it to feel true and to reach your reader's heart. Some of yourself *has* to go onto the page. Consider, however, that selecting a plot that comes close to your experience—one that harnesses the Universal Emotional Truth of that experience without duplicating it entirely— might give you the best shot at success.

Tactic 4: Gain an Editorial Perspective When Writing Nonfiction

What if you're writing a memoir or nonfiction, and what you want to recount is *exactly* what you've experienced? Even this has pitfalls.

When I was writing *Becoming a Chief Home Officer*, I wrote an opening chapter that recounted my harrowing launch into at-home motherhood. The experience involved not only my exit from the workforce and the high-trauma birth of my son, but also my mother's subsequent heart attack when she came to visit the newborn. That event was pretty much a disaster wrapped inside a crisis. I wrote about the darkness of that first scary night in the neonatal intensive care unit after his breathing had finally been stabilized, the terrifying thought that oxygen deprivation had done damage we hadn't yet discovered, and the bleary-eyed sleeplessness of his first colicky nights at home. I recounted the stress of my mom's visit, the growing awareness that she wasn't okay, the last-ditch attempts to get her on a plane home to her own doctors, and the horrible moment when she collapsed in the airport. She survived, thankfully, but spent an additional three weeks at my house recovering alongside a very cranky baby boy and an increasingly frustrated big sister. Trauma on an epic scale! I thought the chapter was dramatic and compelling, and that it would vault the reader right into my high-stress world in the first weeks away from my former career.

My editor wrote a single line at the end of that chapter:

"Now that we've gotten that out of our system, let's start the book with Chapter 2."

Ouch. A painful critique, but true. What the reader needed to know about those difficult weeks could have been summed up in two paragraphs—not an entire bleak, traumatic, blackly detailed chapter. After all, the book's subtitle was *Thriving in Your New Career as a Stay-at-Home Mom.* Again—here's another case for why you *absolutely need an editor* to attempt this kind of writing. My opening chapters went far beyond the needed backstory, straying miles off topic from what the reader wanted from my book. Those experiences felt so real, so cathartic to write, that I could not see it. I was too immersed in the history to judge its importance (or lack thereof).

I've learned to think of packing a suitcase as the metaphor for my nonfiction work: Lay out all of what you think you need to communicate, and then select half of it to take along. The same measure of Universal Truth we talked about earlier applies powerfully even in nonfiction. Think about what it is you want your reader to come away with, and peel away the stories and descriptions that don't point toward that truth (no matter how good they feel to write). You're a human being with highly tuned descriptive powers, so you'll want to tell all of it—every single powerful detail—because it's all important to you. You may have to *write* all of it, as I did the chapter I described above, but remind yourself you shouldn't *use* all of it. I'm going to say it one more time: You need the objectivity of an editor.

> Think about what it is you want your reader to come away with, and peel away the stories and descriptions that don't point toward that truth.

If it helps to convince you, think of the last time you talked to someone in the midst of a crisis. You likely received a whopping dose of TMI—Too Much Information. Oversharing is easy to forgive when it comes from someone you care about, since you were lending a supportive ear at a difficult time. Your reader is different. TMI is likely to make them put the book down, robbing you both of the magic of connecting.

Bonus Tactic: Find Your Armadillo

One benefit of personal experience is a solid collection of realistic coping mechanisms in the face of challenges. The blessing of most traumas is often the deep connections we make with other people in the midst of the difficulties. Your nonfiction should offer practical tips and tactics—those emotional vitamins we covered in Chapter 1. Your fictional plot can also be filled with emotional vitamins to help your characters face up to their challenges—like my family's chocolate cake celebrations. The good news is, you likely now possess a rich trove of relationship moments and acts of kindness that you can now pass on in your writing.

So what's with the armadillo? My son became fascinated with the little armor-plated beasts when he was in grade school, and as such, we happened to have a stuffed armadillo lying around the house—lying around the house for many years, actually, so that it eventually ended up in the "going to charity" box that sits by our back door. One day Charlene, a writer friend of mine, was having a terrible time of it—one of those patches when things totally out of her control were making her miserable, and there was nothing for it but to endure.

On pure impulse (or the nudging of the Spirit, if you believe in such things as I do), I picked up the silly toy and took it with me as I left to meet her for lunch. "Here," I said as I sat down opposite her weary face. "There's nothing to do but hug an armadillo."

It was just silly enough to make her laugh, but the notion stuck. "Hug the armadillo" became a code word of sorts for any issue too big to fix, any problem without a quick solution, or any overwhelming sadness. Now, Charlene is just the kind of person to take an emotional vitamin and turn it into a full-on feast, so she has passed the notion on in her own speaking career. As a matter of fact, at last count, *hundreds* of people have hugged the armadillo. That small ball of stuffing has been squished by scores of folks in crisis and sent on more missions of mercy than I ever could have imagined! He has traveled across the country, ministered from the podium, been prayed over, passed around, and cuddled by countless arms. Did some version of that silly but potent touchstone make it into one of my novels? You betcha. Part of it shows up in the prayer shawl ministries that are an ongoing theme in my Gordon Falls series. I tell the armadillo story often when I speak, as does Charlene. When I have a character in crisis and I need to connect them to their community so that coping and healing can happen, I always think: *Where is their armadillo, and who's going to give it to them?*

Dig through your own experiences to find your armadillos and put them to work on behalf of your character's emotional journey. It's one of the best ways to let your own story imbue your writing with strong, creative details that will make it come alive.

> If the best writing comes from true life, a difficult time can indeed be a trove of great inspiration.

When plotting your fiction, don't just give an armadillo; take it away too. Create a dark moment for your character by removing the "armadillo" that has helped them to cope. Or create a dynamic moment of victory by having your character reach the point of transformation where their coping takes place—the moment when your character passes along their "armadillo" or realizes it's no longer needed. The resolution will be satisfying for your readers. The object— or whatever form your emotional vitamin takes—gives a concrete element to show alongside the emotions you describe and adds a powerful dimension to the narrative. As writers, we want to create characters our readers will love and cheer on. We want our readers to share the moment of victory when the hero or heroine realizes their own conquest over the harrowing conflicts we've thrown at them. Utilizing emotional vitamins can help us achieve that goal.

If the best writing comes from true life, a difficult time can indeed be a trove of great inspiration. The trick comes in knowing how to wisely mine your life for the deep truths that can give significance to your work. If you use the tactics we've covered, I hope you will be able to use your struggles to impact your work, filling the sails of your writing vessel to go to great places.

In the next chapter, we'll look at some similar issues for those of you who also speak or teach.

Chapter 5

Light a Beacon: When to Speak

Many of us who write—especially those of us who write nonfiction—augment our writing careers with speaking engagements. Whether as a keynote at a writers' event, teaching, book signings, or conferences, people love to hear about the personal experience behind the written words. Just as in writing, there are elements of such highly personal speaking that should be considered before you step up to the podium.

The issues deserve careful consideration because of the real-time nature of speaking. We can edit chapters or scenes, but second takes don't often happen on the speaker's dais. How can you use the powerful platform of speaking to support and expand your writing career while avoiding its pitfalls? Use these tactics to ensure your experience is a good one for both you and your audience.

Tactic 1: Decide If You're Ready

Today's world offers a wide range of options for sharing your story. You can tell it any number of ways to any number of people. That's good, but it also reminds me of an old adage: Just because you *can* doesn't necessarily mean you *should*.

So how do you know if you *should*? How can you evaluate when and if you're ready?

A. Do you know the Universal Truth yet?

If you don't—and almost no one does in the midst of the crisis—you're not ready to speak. Talking about it in social or even recovery settings like support groups is fine, but resist getting behind the podium until you know you have something concrete to offer a wider audience. Take that "gotta do something with it" energy and channel it into digging up and refining those Universal Truths.

B. Talk to someone who is already doing it.

> ...resist getting behind the podium until you know you have something concrete to offer a wider audience.

Seek the wise counsel of someone who is already speaking about a traumatic experience or adversity. There may be parts of the experience you don't know are coming, which may help you realize you are either ready or need more time. Tell your story to that experienced person and ask for their advice. Feel free to consult with people whose experience is different from yours, for much of this translates across any number of adversities; but make sure that you also look for those with experience close to yours. Seeing who is out there already speaking on the topic you have in mind may gain you useful insight.

C. Send up a trial balloon.

Start talking about it. Write a blog post or the first chapter. Share what you have in mind with colleagues. If you already have a speaking or writing career, begin including that topic on your speaking menu or project list. If it sparks interest, you will know you are onto something, and you can decide if it is time to take the work to a more concrete level. This entire book happened because I included "Writing through Adversity" on my speaking topic list. When hosts began asking for the presentation, I knew things were ready to come to fruition.

D. Engage in prayer or meditation.

If you are a person of faith, now is a very good time to call upon that faith. Spend time in prayer or meditation over your desire to tell your story, over the lessons you've learned, and over the people who might benefit from those lessons. Ask those close to you to pray that you will receive answers, and start looking for those answers to appear. You may indeed get a clear yes or no from the process, or conclusions may elude you. No matter what, make sure either your spirituality or deliberate and thoughtful consideration plays a key role in your decision.

E. Remember: "No" is really more like "Not now."

If your efforts go nowhere, trust that the story hasn't quite found its time. Trust that you have some more work to do, that you need more distance and perspective. The response you receive is not a negation of your experience or a devaluation of what you have to say. Your story isn't meaningless; it's just not fully ready to meet the wider world.

If your efforts go nowhere, trust that the story hasn't quite found its time.

Tactic 2: Learn How to Manage Strong Emotions

If you're going to share, you're likely going to cry. Or at least choke up.

If you share your work and lessons in a public forum, parts of it will rise up with strong emotional power. That's not a bad thing; it means you've dug deep enough and been brave enough to put the essential truths out there for your audience.

But let's take a moment to get real: Most of us don't look like cinema stars when we tear up. Our voices squeak, our noses run, we lose our trains of thought, or any number of other less-than-elegant outcomes. This is especially true if you are "a crier" like me. Movies, stories, important moments, television commercials, even greeting cards can trigger my waterworks. That's as much a hindrance as it is an asset.

The tradition in our church is for the senior class to give the Youth Sunday sermon. My son (who may have his mama's public presence, after all) was chosen to give a major portion of the message. Before he said one word, he stepped down off the pulpit and walked into the pews to hand me a box of tissues. What can I say? The boy knows his mom. Yes, his story is particularly compelling because of all he's been through, but his mom is also particularly prone to tears. The funny, poignant moment launched a most memorable speech by someone about to vault off to college. I doubt I'll ever forget it.

And yes, I cried. Tears, after all, aren't bad. They shouldn't be avoided. I always connect strongly with a speaker who is choking up because I know it means their message is from their deepest experience. Powerful emotions make for a powerful message. If you can't talk about it without crying, I consider that a sign that deep truths are at work and making their way to your audience. I like it. I value it. I encourage it.

Out-of-control emotions, however, make everyone uncomfortable. Sobbing at the podium is hard to watch, even if we sympathize with the speaker. The trick for you is to figure out how to tap into that emotion without taking yourself to a place where you lose all composure. Here are a few tips I've learned from experience and other speakers.

A. Tell the story out loud repeatedly and in private.

...figure out how to tap into that emotion without taking yourself to a place where you lose all composure.

I will rehearse the difficult parts of a message over and over at home, in the car (when safe, of course), or anywhere I can get the words out. And by out, I mean *out loud*. The first time will undoubtedly take you to into a major cry. The second and third times, you will likely discover a bit more control. You're not exactly *rehearsing*—more like *conditioning*. You'll discover phrases that help you and images you should embrace or pull away from. The process will encourage your emotional self to generally get comfortable with the telling.

B. Look up and breathe.

Look up, but not at the audience—because chances are they're tearing up right alongside you. Find a focus that will not emote back at you and stay there for a minute or so until you can return to your audience's faces. Looking down tends to make it worse—I don't really know why—but looking up cues your body to rise and steady itself.

C. Plan how you'll get out of it.

Every story will have the point, the detail, the plot turn that takes it to the darkest moment. If you have gotten familiar with your speech, you'll develop a sense of where that "cry point" is. Plan ahead for how you'll move yourself and your audience forward. For me, it is almost always a joke, even if it's something as basic as: "And that, ladies and gentlemen, is why they make waterproof mascara." Think of it as a verbal lifeline you throw yourself in your sea of tears. Go ahead and go deep, but have a few tactics ready for how to pull yourself back to shore.

Go ahead and go deep, but have a few tactics ready for how to pull yourself back to shore.

D. Be selective with your stories.

Not every story has to be told. Some stories are too crushing to parade out in public. Parts of my mother's death, my son's illness, or any other of my life's darker moments will never come to the podium. It's not that they are wrong, or that they can't teach valuable lessons; it's just that I'm not prepared to visit those particular places repeatedly in front of an audience. Just because you speak or write doesn't mean you are obligated to display your entire emotional self for the world to see.

Tactic 3: Develop Emotional Fortitude

Taking your story public demands a certain type of courage and confidence. Yes, you must be willing to be vulnerable and open, but you also will want to acquire what I call *emotional fortitude*. More than a thick skin, emotional fortitude is the ability to withstand the inevitable slings and arrows that will come your way once you make a private experience public.

Such obstacles could be a reason to decline writing or speaking about your experience. Deciding you're not willing to expose yourself to the ramifications is a perfectly valid (some might even say wise) response to the adversity in your life. But like a certain superhero has always said, "With great exposure comes great responsibility." Okay, he put it a little differently, but you get my point. Here are a few ways to gauge if your emotional armor is firmly in place.

A. Decide if you are strong enough for pushback.

Not everyone will agree with you. They may find your choices different from theirs, or they may disagree with your decision to "go public." We all hope our friends admire the choice we've made to share our experience and offer wisdom, encouragement, and support to others. Yet it doesn't always turn out that way. "Why did you have to tell everyone?" "You're capitalizing on what's happened to you!" "You just want the attention." "What makes you an expert?" are all things I've heard to my face—both from people who know me well and from complete strangers. Even when you know to expect it, it's startling. And unnerving. If you know it's coming, you can better arm yourself with replies. You can also have your friends at the ready to commiserate with you and keep you on track.

B. Ask yourself: "Am I ready to offer my arm to others?"

When you choose to speak publicly, it's no longer just about your story. You will hear many stories of similar, related, or even entirely different experiences. (This will also happen if you write about your struggle, by the way.) We all want to tell our stories to people who will understand; it's human nature. Each person reaching out to you deserves your attention and response (except for the nasty ones. I give you permission to ignore those!). Every single time I speak on my experiences I expect—and make time for—people who want to talk afterward. This means scheduling reaction time in a workshop setting, making sure I have a volunteer at my book table so I can talk instead of making transactions, walking through the audience after a presentation, and other tactics. Connecting with the audience often requires digging deep into energy stores that are usually depleted by speaking. And I confess, such connections did not come naturally to me at first. The rewards, however, are rich and encouraging.

When the events of 9/11 spurred me to write *Facing Every Mom's Fears*, I experienced a deluge of maternal anxiety stories in letters, in emails, and after presentations. Some of them were funny and warmly touching, while others were downright gut-wrenching. Part of my new role continues to be listening to, praying with, and encouraging these moms. I take time to offer suggestions or to be a sympathetic ear. This dynamic has become an inextricable part of taking my story public. I should have expected it and prepared for it, but I didn't; and it took me several months to gain enough footing to carry on in strength and wisdom.

C. Make sure you can acquire distance when you need it.

Hearing everyone's life traumas is emotionally exhausting. If we engaged on a full intimate and emotional level with all of our audiences, we'd be rubbed raw from human contact. If your own wounds or the chaos of your experience are too fresh, you may not be able to develop the emotional distance between yourself and your audience that is necessary to keep going. I'm not saying be aloof or unsympathetic—that would be disingenuous at best and wrong at worst—but make sure you are able to pull back and disengage yourself from others' problems and the reliving of your own. If you have recently lost your spouse, for example, are you ready to recount the experience and hear others' experiences of that dark valley over and over? Can you plan for ways to replenish your soul and spirit so that your audience's fresh grief doesn't overwhelm your own grief process? Give thought to this now, before your story is out there, so that you can connect without being consumed.

> ...make sure you are able to pull back and disengage yourself from others' problems and the reliving of your own.

If you give thought to these issues now, your speaking platform can be one of the most powerful ways to strengthen your writing career. It can—and has for me—become one of the most rewarding outcomes of any adversity. My speaking platform is a priceless source of support, affirmation, outreach, and encouragement. You owe yourself that opportunity, but you also owe yourself the proper protections and support systems to ensure that your willingness to "put yourself out there" is a choice you don't regret.

Chapter 6

Launch Your Vessel: Where Do I Go from Here?

You have worked through the process of preparing, and now you feel ready to utilize your adversity in your writing life. You've mined your experience for its treasures, discovered ways to connect with audiences, and armed yourself for the challenges ahead. What's the next step? How do you answer the question, "Are you going to write about this?"

Let's take a look at the ways you can set things in motion on a project that is now calling to you based on your experience.

Tactic 1: Take These Steps
If the Response Is "Start Now"

I do believe your own sense of creativity will tell you when you are ready to write about whatever you've faced or are facing. An opportunity may present itself before you feel ready. Or you may be ready, but no opportunity appears on your horizon. The decision to put the traumas of your life on paper involves a balancing act of internal and external factors that will be different for every writer.

When you and the world are ready, here are some steps to take.

A. Read through your journals.

When we were new parents, we observed our children and often thought, *I'll never, ever forget this!*—only to realize later that the details had slipped through our memories. As you prepare to tell your story, scour your journals from before, during, and after your crisis to find the potent details, the emotional vitamins, the small victories, and the dark hours. How you feel as you read them may tell you a great deal about how truly ready you are to spend a lot of time revisiting a difficult period. Simply put, use yourself as research.

> When you begin writing, be prepared for your creative speed to disobey you.

Go through your emails, social media, greeting cards—anything that can offer detailed peeks into the path you trod. If you used a communication site like CaringBridge or Facebook, many of these services offer to compile all the notes of encouragement and cries for help into a commemorative volume. I found this especially useful. If you don't have many written accounts, perhaps the first step is to get your memories and reactions down on paper.

B. Respect the gush...or the trickle.

When you begin writing, be prepared for your creative speed to disobey you. You may find that opening up the emotional floodgates results in huge stockpiles of words. The next day—or the next month—you may find things going very slowly. I have found it unwise to force things.

Your subconscious knows more about what you're ready to face than your conscious mind does. Trust your individual process and progress. Nudge it along if you'd like, but resist forcing anything.

C. Identify your primary Universal Truth.

Perhaps you've uncovered multiple Universal Truths for the writing you want to do. That's great, but too many themes can pull your focus in too many directions. Take time to ponder, and to consult others who have been through something similar. Also talk with those who haven't been anywhere close to the valley you've walked. See where the connections lie, see what stories people relate to most strongly, and decide which lessons are the most powerful. Keep at it until one or two Universal Truths emerge as the focus or theme your writing needs.

D. Decide if you will pursue fiction or nonfiction.

If you, like me, have skills in both genres, you have a decision to make. I've chosen to reflect my experiences in fiction up until this book, but I have also spoken frequently about my experiences. Part of this stems from the truth that I'm not the only person in this story; my son and the rest of my family have privacy and opinions that deserve respect. For now, I've chosen to let the nonfiction, memoir-style account wait until I feel I and my family are ready. That may be next year, a few years from now, or never. Many writers with powerful life stories have shared how difficult it is for a "noncelebrity" to publish a memoir through traditional routes. This is why independent publishing has seen a surge of such books. Perhaps try your hand at some fiction and some memoir or nonfiction, and then see what feels like the best fit. I absolutely believe truths can be taught directly or in story with equal power.

> I absolutely believe truths can be taught directly or in story with equal power.

E. Consider that your story might not be a book.

The good news is that these days, you can reach readers in so many ways. Yes, books often come to mind first, but what about magazine articles? Blogs? Podcasts? If your urge is to be heard, to share your story, today's digital universe offers you many ways to connect with others. If you are especially interested in nonfiction, a blog serves as an excellent place to get your feet wet, to find readers, and to build that all-important "platform" publishers want to see. The feedback you get from some of these outlets can provide a vital sense of how it feels to "go public" on a small and protectable scale.

Tactic 2: Take These Steps If the Response Is "Not Now"

It's difficult to see doors shut in your face when you've decided you are ready to share your powerful experience. As a person of faith, I trust that those doors shut for a reason, but that doesn't make it any easier to accept the walls that rise up in front of a project I feel strongly about. You may send out trial inquiries, only to get no response—an outcome that can feel even worse than rejection. As I mentioned earlier, memoirs are notoriously hard sells in today's traditional market, so multiple publishers may decline your queries. You may receive pushback or even outright resistance from friends and family members who are involved or related to your experience. Your agent may tell you to "put this project away for a while." Events out of your control may create the wrong atmosphere for your story or message. The publishing world is very good at saying no; and while I always look at "no" as "not now," that perspective rarely makes rejection any easier to swallow. Here are some tips to try if you find yourself in the challenge of waiting.

A. Write to *process*, not to publish.

Even if the time is not right, there's no reason why you can't start a project anyway—as long as you keep your goals appropriate. You will learn so much in that first draft that if your heart is telling you it's time, go for it. Get it down on paper—whatever it is. In the past I have started a book only to discover the project is really a *different* book, but I had to get knee-deep in the first idea to discover the second. Record the stories or scenes that are coming to you now, realizing they may only be seeds to future stories or scenes. Just because the world isn't ready doesn't mean you aren't ready.

B. Strengthen your trust and patience muscles.

Yes, I am fully aware that being patient is easier said than done. If you are a person of faith, now is the time to dig deep into the spirituality of your circumstance. Remind yourself of other times in your life when your personal timetable failed—and especially remind yourself of the times when what did finally happen was far better than your original plan. Read biographies of people whose patience and perseverance are admirable and worth emulating. Talk to other writers and commiserate. Look for ready projects right in front of you that you can pick up while you wait for this one to find its time.

C. Stockpile memories, scenes, and thoughts.

Write—just don't write to publish. Write to record, knowing that one idea or memory often spurs more. Think of your writing as building a stockpile for that time when the project does come to fruition. You'll be in great shape as you pore over your ready inventory, pulling the very best material for your project once you get the green light. Trust that the additional time will give you even sharper perspective to choose the best material from everything you've gathered.

D. Share interpersonally.

I'm not talking about the podium here; I'm talking about *talking*. Conversation in groups or one-on-one. Okay, you raging introverts, I get that this is a tough one. Extroverts, you're probably already doing this (and, if you're like me, maybe even too much of this). The point is to tell the story out loud as well as on paper. As you share with people, you will discover new lessons, fresh perspectives, and points that touch others' hearts in ways you hadn't even expected. I was one of the first persons in my friend group to be a parent, one of very few to endure the serious illness of a child, and one of the first to go through the battlefield of elder-care. Talking about it gave me additional writing material—both in my fiction and nonfiction. Connections to other people deepened the well of experiences I could draw from to create characters different from myself. Sharing stories gave me new viewpoints to include in nonfiction.

E. Consider a blog.

Blogging, like self-publishing, is both a welcome outlet and a danger zone. Though I'm often the person to stomp my feet and decide to do something anyway even when I've heard a "not yet," there are too many times when I've regretted it. Force yourself to hear the reasons you are receiving nos or not yets. Most of the time they are

> If you need to be heard, blogging or independent publishing can be a great way to do so.

valid. At the very least, you should choose to go forward with your eyes completely open to the reasons behind the resistance. If you need to be heard, blogging or independent publishing can be a great way to do so. I would caution you in the strongest possible terms, however, to ensure that all privacy and confidentiality issues have been resolved before moving forward.

Final Thoughts: Stones and Pearls

It's hard to write when life is hard. Still, it's worth doing—even if circumstances have given you no choice. Writing that comes from a difficult season is valuable. Worthwhile. Striving to create those words is an honorable deed.

One of my favorite metaphors for this comes from the biblical story of Joshua. As he finally led his people over the Jordan River and into the promised land, the passage marked the end of one of history's greatest epics and decades of hardship, trauma, and danger. The event is worth not just one book, but several (at least in biblical terms, not to mention a host of great Hollywood movies).

As he crossed the Jordan—his finish line, if you will—Joshua was instructed to have the priests who were standing in the middle of the river reach down and pick up a stone from the riverbed. They reached down to the dry ground God had created in the middle of all that rushing water and plucked a souvenir to take with them to the other side. A stone of remembrance, a physical reminder of the exodus now (hopefully) behind them.

I think it's important to note that the stone was from the *middle* of the river, not the victorious final shore. The totems came from right inside the mess, symbols of a moment when life hadn't worked itself out yet. See your "Jordan stones" for the treasures they are. Pick them up, pile them where you and others can see them, and use them as reminders of your past, present, and future journey.

The totems came from right inside the mess, symbols of a moment when life hadn't worked itself out yet.

The pearl is another fitting symbol for the message of this entire book. You may have heard the saying: "You can't get a pearl without a little grit." It's true that a pearl is beauty borne of an irritant—the product of time coating an invasive grain one thin, shiny layer at a time. When I find myself writing about the crises, traumas, and challenges of my life, each word coats the pearl. Each speech adds to its unique luster. I couldn't do life any other way. Neither, I suspect, could you.I've heard more than one writer say, "It's all material." It's true. All of life is indeed material for those of us born with the need to tell stories, to create from our experiences. That's the gift of a creative personality. Our nature is not something to be tamped down or stifled.Our craft is, however, something to be honed and polished. I hope this book has given you the tools you need to take whatever grit has invaded your life and transform it into a pearl. An object of beauty, unique in all the world to your experience and the luster you add. It's my fervent prayer that I've given you ways to look at your experience so that good comes from bad, sharing eases the burden, and harm gives way to hope.The world needs your story. Maybe the whole wide world, or maybe just your corner of it. Maybe now, or maybe years from now. Maybe in a completely different way than you first imagined. If I've helped you even a few steps along that journey, then this book will have done the job I sent it out into the world to do.

Dear Reader,

My hope is that this book has given you true help during a tough time. As one of our most important assets as writers, our creativity deserves protection. I want to see you finding ways to stay the writer you are, even when life's chaos seems determined to squash your muse.

I'd love to hear from you. Email me at allie@alliepleiter.com and tell me what you've faced or are facing, and how you have learned to cope. I welcome your success stories and tales of failed attempts. The more we share, the stronger we become as a community of writers.

If you haven't already, I hope you'll check out my other book for writers, *The Chunky Method Handbook: Your Step-by-Step Plan to FINISH THAT BOOK Even When Life Gets in the Way*. You'll find that many Chunky Method strategies complement those you learned in this book.

One of my favorite things to do is to connect face-to-face (or screen-to-screen), teaching these and other topics. If you have a retreat, a local writing group, a writers' conference, or another event, visit *alliepleiter.com/speaking.html* and let's talk.

Here are all the ways you can connect with me:
- Instagram: @alliepleiterauthor
- Facebook: @alliepleiter

- Twitter: @alliepleiter
- Pinterest: @alliepleiter
- Goodreads: ***goodreads.com/alliepleiter***

Until me meet again—on the page or in person—keep writing!

—Allie

Printed in Great Britain
by Amazon